WILDLIFE IN BLOOM SERIES

Little Frog

BY AUTHOR & CONSERVATIONIST

LINDA BLACKMOOR

ISBN: 978-1-966417-21-7 (PRINT)

PUBLISHED BY QUILL PRESS. LINDA BLACKMOOR'S TITLES MAY BE
PURCHASED IN BULK FOR EDUCATIONAL, BUSINESS, FUNDRAISING, OR
SALES PROMOTIONAL USE. FOR INFORMATION, PLEASE EMAIL
HELLO@LINDABLACKMOOR.COM

FIRST PRINT EDITION: 2025

LINDA BLACKMOOR
WWW.LINDABLACKMOOR.COM

FROG FACTS #1

SPECIES

Frogs are amphibians (order of Anura), with over 7,000 species found on every continent except Antarctica. Their close relatives include toads, but the difference is that toads typically have drier, bumpier skin. Frogs vary in size from the tiny Paedophryne amauensis, measuring under half an inch, to the hefty Goliath frog, which can grow over a foot long. Each species has unique colors, patterns, and calls.

LIFE

Frogs have a two-stage life cycle, beginning as aquatic tadpoles before transforming into air-breathing adults. Tadpoles typically have tails and gills, swimming like fish while they grow legs and lose their tails. After metamorphosis, adult frogs spend more time on land, although many still stay near water. This remarkable change is controlled by hormones.

SKIN

Frog skin is thin and porous, allowing them to breathe through it and absorb water directly. This means they don't have to drink water like we do, but it also makes them sensitive to pollution and chemicals. Some frogs have special glands that produce toxins, protecting them from predators. Bright colors often warn enemies of their poisonous nature, while dull tones help with camouflage.

CALLS

Male frogs attract mates or defend territory with vocal calls, which come from a sac in their throat that inflates like a balloon. Each species has its own call, helping females find the right kind of frog in a chorus of croaks. Calling often happens at night, when the air is cooler and safer from daytime predators. Certain species can even make calls underwater by letting sound vibrations travel through water.

JUMP

Frogs are famous for their jump, using strong back legs to leap far beyond their body length. The tiny tree frog can jump around 20 times its own size, while large species like the bullfrog still spring several feet. Elastic tendons in the legs store energy like a spring, releasing it quickly for a powerful launch. This acrobatic ability helps frogs catch food or escape hungry predators in a single bound.

DIET

Most adult frogs are carnivores, eating insects, spiders, worms, and even small fish or other frogs. They have long, sticky tongues that can flick out in an instant to snatch prey. Some larger species, such as the African bullfrog, can take down small mammals or birds. By controlling bug populations, frogs help keep ecosystems in balance.

HABITAT

Frogs live in a variety of habitats, from tropical rainforests and swamps to deserts and even mountains. They stay near water sources for breeding, since eggs and tadpoles need moisture to survive. Arboreal frogs use sticky pads on their toes to cling to leaves and branches high above the ground. Despite living in many environments, most frogs rely on moisture to keep their skin healthy.

COLORS

Frog colors range from bright blues, reds, and yellows to plain browns and greens. Vibrant poison dart frogs warn predators they're toxic, while mossy-colored frogs blend into forest floors to hide. Seasonal or mood changes can slightly alter their shade, helping them regulate temperature or communicate. Some glass frogs even have see-through skin, revealing their internal organs.

HIBERNATE

In colder regions, frogs enter hibernation, burying themselves in mud or leaf litter to wait out winter. Their bodies slow down, and they rely on stored energy reserves until spring arrives. Aquatic species sometimes rest in the water's depths, where the temperature stays above freezing. This strategy allows them to survive harsh conditions and emerge when food is plentiful again.

FROG FACTS #10

SONGS

Frogs are known for their choruses, with multiple males calling at once, creating a nightly symphony by ponds and rivers. Each frog's unique pitch and rhythm help females identify the strongest mate. During breeding season, these choruses can be heard from far away, guiding others to good gathering spots. Some frogs sing so loudly, it can be difficult for humans to sleep nearby!

CHANGE

The change from tadpole to frog is called metamorphosis, which takes weeks or months depending on the species and environment. Tadpoles develop lungs to breathe air, and their tails gradually shrink while legs grow in. Hormones control when and how this transformation happens, ensuring it lines up with food availability and safe conditions. By the end, a fully formed frog emerges, ready to explore.

FROG FACTS #12

POISON

Many frogs produce poisons in their skin, especially bright-colored ones like poison dart frogs in Central and South America. Their toxins can cause numbness, illness, or even death to predators that try to eat them. Indigenous hunters once tipped blow darts with these potent chemicals, showing how powerful frog poison can be. Not all colorful frogs are toxic, but most are best left untouched.

FROG FACTS #13

PARENTS

Some frogs display extraordinary parental care, going far beyond laying eggs in water. The Surinam toad carries eggs on its back, where they sink into the skin until the babies hatch. Darwin's frog fathers guard eggs in their vocal sacs, shielding the tadpoles until they are ready to hop away. This devoted parenting style helps ensure more tadpoles survive in challenging environments.

www.ingramcontent.com/pod-product-compliance
Lightning Source LLC
Chambersburg PA
CBHW060837270326
41933CB00002B/115